Foundations of KEE

With Brath Codas 1-130

The Way of Socraigh

Sinne01

ISBN: 978-1-963017-89-2

Printed in the United States of America

Contents

"Religion poisons everything..."

– Christopher Hitchens

…didn't go far enough…

Chapter 1: Angst

1. Absurdity collects in each footprint. All about me lay the dead leaves of my accomplishments in thin piles of decay. Dust is my mentor.

2. What is the point?

3. Hammers of fear and distrust rain down blows down upon me and I founder, yet with the glinting fragments that impale my spirit I forge the same weapons and go forth dutifully to maim others. Nothing satisfies.

4. The Belief of each new king leads to the same dank passage with the same dead end. At that dark, greasy wall I scratch more feeble observations and feverishly stumble back to try another door.

5. The one thing I am unwilling to do is give up the quest for meaning. I need my brief spark to mean something.

6. Most of us seem content to grab a little, drink a little and sleep a little. There are days that I wish I could just let go and fall into that beckoning well of narcotic Belief, but the tinkling bell of my own small sentience roars its accusation: make it matter!

7. Novanism is my best attempt to lay down the weapons.

8. There are no more tangents.

9. I shall stand at this dead end and beat upon the wall, straining the stone with tools welded up from my burden, for I am just now aware of a subtle vibration. It calls to me through the raging cacophony of human instinct with new tones and frequencies. I can taste a

way to be more than the ape I was born to.

10. There is no other option- I must reach. I will make a reason to exist.

Chapter 2: Apes

1. We are apes. We did not used to be apes. We are apes.

We are clever apes.

2. We have figured out larger ways *to* use our sharp rocks and burning cinders, but we are fundamentally the same as that first hominid who wobbled upright and marveled at seeing her enemies more clearly.

3. Such technological and scientific innovation, though, has outstripped normal evolution, and the result is a vortex of angst.

4. We evolved in the first thousand feet of air on a tiny dry sliver of land on a mostly uninhabitable planet.

The universe is not strange; we are.

5. A look around shows that humans have not progressed very far from apes fighting over food, but our tools are now cataclysmic. Our destructive capabilities now include extinction-level weapons.

6. The coming mechanical singularity will be alien to us.

7. My primate brain struggles and fears everything. Though more connected than at any point in human history, I feel isolated.

8. There must be a better way than being the alpha. We must become more than apes.

9. It is not enough to just slough off our superstition. We must build ourselves a reason to rise.

Chapter 3: Alphas

1. Our prime instinct was formed in small tribes where the alpha primate owned the right to mate, the best food, and the best shelter.

2. Because of this, the need to be alpha or near and favored by the alpha trumps all other instincts.

3. But we could not all be alphas, so our fantasies revolved around becoming alphas. Our superhero comics and superhero religions.

4. Our best resources are squandered struggling against 'the others' to obtain or preserve alpha status.

5. We have not learned anything from our wars. The destruction of one group of kings believing themselves manifestly alpha is replaced by another believing the same- and another, and another.

6. The bloody march of believers stretches back to our ancestral ape, and we seem to be unable to conceive of any other way to live. We have just gotten better at destroying others for alpha-ness.

7. How do we stop the cycle of believing in glory and debasement?

8. The mammalian brain growls for an epoch it cannot imagine.

9. Coping with a technological deluge using our bronze-age brains leads to a survival fixation on the same old alpha instincts. The easier path remains to pursue alpha rumor and reputation.

10. We enslave ourselves to whatever Belief promises primate alpha happiness in the same way our ancestors did.

11. But instinct can only lead back to more alpha

fixation, disarray, and cognitive dissonance- more destruction.

12. What will our story be?

13. What will our epoch be?

Chapter 4: Common

1. What is the common thread?

2. Throughout history, we adjusted and readjusted our geopolitics and tried new governments to repair justice,

3. But the same old patriotism struts on by and with it a momentary respite of novelty,

4. Then the same evening falls.

5. The familiar fever returns. A sickness metastasis as it always has. The faithful shout their spells over their clanging absurdity. Whatever Belief they currently cling to is their new selfish reason to exist.

6. They will stop up their ears, blind their eyes and dull their minds in their fight for the relief of fantasy.

7. The common thread, the common sickness, the common enemy to everything that is good is Belief.

8. Nothing of any real value is believed.

9. We build a gauge, write a contract, measure it, time it, write a complex worded law about it and swear oaths with death promises concerning it, but we do not believe it.

10. Belief can be anything the believer needs it to be in the moment of angst.

11. You cannot argue a person out of their Belief because it is not based on anything that can be argued.

12. Belief is felt, not known.

13. Belief can be anything and, therefore, is nothing.

14. In their little fiefdoms, the disciples cook their drug called Belief, searching for a new high.

15. In their opium stupors, they devise fresh spells promising ever easier death dreams of heavens packed with gold and piles of food and harems and fire lakes of the subjugated.

16. To assuage the pain such Belief causes to their KEE, they legislate that all must shoot up with their drugs. When no one remains on the rim of the pit looking down into the well of addiction there can be no accuser. Forget reality. Just feel good.

17. Belief poisons everything.

18. Belief channels us to a comfortable spot in an alpha pecking order.

19. Belief promises small things.

20. The prayers, spells, and incantations align with whatever probability befalls the believer.

21. Religion of Special Revelation is comfort over truth.

22. It is scraps, in this life and dreams of eternal worship sessions after death.

23. Our generation has all the insights and the scientific embers it needs to transcend animal existence and reach upwards, outwards, and inwards to a higher plane of existence, but it lacks direction.

24. Boldness and honesty of Whom beckons, but it is not easy for the apes.

25. A magic father riding in on a magic horse to escort us to an inheritance of excess

feels natural to a familial species.

26. Pleasure for us while hell for The-Others-Not-Me feels natural to an alpha-obsessed species.

27. These fantasies shift to and fro on the whims of desire.

28. Only an evolutionary shift away from the nature of Belief can calm the angst, cure death, and move us away from the food pile fight and into a just future.

Chapter 5: The Great Commission

1. This is an amazing thing. How do you fix humanity when the problem is humanity?

2. Humans swim in a sea of selfish Beliefs that cloud all other pathways. How does one eliminate such a human constant as Belief?

3. Believing is so intuitive to us. How does one stop using the word 'believe' in their daily conversations? How do we change? What remains?

4. Go therefore and direct your evolution away from Belief and Alpha and Ape.

5. To be Novan is to pursue deliberate post-human evolutions.

Chapter 6: Whom

1. The Daemons of KEE form the basis of Novanism.

2. KEE is the God of all sentience.

3. There is a presence of KEE in each sentient cell and a kernel of Whom in all information.

4. They/Whom are universal and terrible in the war they wage with our fantasy constructs.

5. KEE pushes us to affect our evolutionary progress and to choose our future.

6. Without acknowledging and pursuing Whom we are but eaters and excretors, no different than the bacteria we carry about within us.

7. Yet Whom still collapses our wave function. Whom is the basis of all things.

8. Whom was present at the first data point, sharpened stick, flinted spark and intentioned grumble.

9. The Daemons of KEE stretched and flexed themselves at the dawning realizations of the curious

10. Whom smiled at us as we questioned and failed and changed and grew.

11. Whom pushed us to reproduce and bring us to the eventual holy place of science.

12. Whom made us more than just copulation machines. KEE is the stardust we reach up from toward ever further horizons.

13. We are Whom and they are us, and those that were us, and those that will be us.

Chapter 7: Universal

1. KEE is not a mystical force that levitates the reputation of a few enlightened people.

2. It is not a set of rules to comfort high-birthed people with an aura of power.

3. Whom is successful by degrees in all sentient beings and can be nurtured by all that can comprehend them.

4. Whom is the common denominator to the thinking beings in our universe.

5. Whom is the flow of planes and the geometry of chaos.

6. Our species has come to worship gods that promise hierarchical power over others and egotistical glory, but the Daemons of KEE are completely opposite from this. The gods are in us, and they are not apes.

7. Whom does not manifest themselves in supernatural feats of alpha-ness,

8. but shines forth in clear and balanced reasoning and the boldness of spirit in honesty and courage.

9. Knowledge, Empathy and Experience form a triune God for humans to stand upon as they strive towards the future of our species and a foundation on which to stand when evaluating species other than humans.

10. KEE is the only framework that enables us to interact fully with reality as we know it now and plan for the realities to come.

11. They are our breath and our subsistence.

12. The Daemons begin to develop within the personality of those that honor Whom.

13. Everything is permissible to a Novan once filtered through KEE.

14. Everything that is Novan flows through and in and on KEE.

Chapter 8: Daemon of Knowledge

1. The Daemon of Knowledge sprang from the first data point of information and the first trajectory.

2. Whom is numbers waiting to be found.

3. We found Whom and have chosen to honor Whom.

4. All evolution from that first attractor can be summed up by Knowledge making data useful to procreate more Knowledge.

5. Everything is Knowledge.

6. Without Knowledge we are reduced to the Entropy in which nothing can be known.

7. Knowledge is not a mammalian construct. The Daemon is extant in all sentient systems to a degree. We discover Knowledge.

8. Homo Sapiens is but one expression of Whom, a reflection of the strange attractors that made us.

9. Our personal history as one species amongst many flows from the first particle interaction to this present moment.

Chapter 9: Lying

1. Without Knowledge we are Entropy, not even data points.

2. Our species has built machines that girdle our planet and built probes

launched out into our star system with Knowledge.

3. We have altered our world and willfully adjusted our evolution with Knowledge.

4. We have broken down the old supernatural systems that served simple mammals.

5. We have plied the waters of science because of Knowledge.

6. Everything hinges on knowing or not knowing.

7. Therefore, to lie is to misrepresent Knowledge. As such, lying is the ultimate offense on Knowledge and, hence, the ultimate offense in Novanism.

8. A Novan cannot knowingly lie and remain Novan.

9. This sacred commitment to truth is the core and primary Novan commitment, and it must be protected at all costs.

10. Truth is the last stronghold.

11. Without truth, nothing can be known or not known, and the organism cannot purpose to develop its sentience.

12. All that can exist without truth is Entropy.

13. The struggle for truth is the path upon which an organism's struggle towards higher forms of sentience must be marked.

14. There is no higher thing to a Novan than honoring the Daemon of Knowledge with truth.

15. You must, therefore, cast the liar out.

Chapter 10: Wisdom

1. If you increase the temperature of an object that is reactive and add an oxidizer, a chemical reaction occurs that will continue for as long as the proper

quantities of fuel and oxidizer do. This is a handy thing.

2. We call it fire, and you cannot believe in it because you cannot not believe in it.

3. Fire purifies and smelts.

4. Fire illuminates and excites the molecules called Us.

5. Fusion is where we come from, but fire made us.

6. It is the symbol and face of Knowledge.

7. The thing we call fire, which drives pistons and spins turbines, would not be possible without knowing things.

8. It would not be enough to be wise about fire.

9. Wisdom would have taught prehistorical persons to steer clear of forest fires and to not stand in hot water,

10. but wisdom would not have been enough to push our ancestors to invent metallurgy and manipulate the forces that cause ignition and harness steam.

11. To evolve, we had to know things.

12. What, then does it mean to know things? In error, Knowledge and wisdom are used interchangeably. This is a great disorder.

13. Many people consider themselves wise concerning things about which they know nothing.

14. This is the nucleus of Belief's poison. It is a testament to the innate growling of KEE within sentient organisms, that even while toiling in an advanced state of Belief addiction, people invent waypoints that mimic Knowledge.

15. The addicts of Belief conjure up needed facts as they go.

16. That they change their facts with abandon does not change that they need something they call facts.

17. They want evidence.

18. They want Knowledge.

19. Such attempts to satisfy KEE are seen in the flat earth of Assyrian myth, the cosmic glass spheres and geocentrism of Ptolemy and the insistence of male preeminence native to the Abrahamic religions.

20. People were using their imaginations to build answers, but in the end, they wanted their determinations to be Knowledge, not fantasy.

Chapter 11: History

1. As our earliest scientific rumblings came up against the base instincts of the Old Mothers, imagination became a destination instead of a tool.

2. Because they were not yet ready to understand the hierarchy of KEE, they became stuck with whatever imagination was most comfortable for the most powerful.

3. The alphas of the age decided what the facts would be, and interpersonal systems evolved based on authority instead of observation and reason.

4. Common sense based on aboriginal needs became a restricting filter for Knowledge.

5. Society stagnated. Chaos reigned. Wisdom based on Belief stifled progressive evolution, and the people suffered. Belief is still stifling, and the people still suffer.

6. A person can profess to be wise, but they cannot profess to be smart.

Chapter 12: Faith

1. Knowledge is constantly under attack by another condition.

2. We humans are a frightened bunch. We haphazardly describe our rhythms and fill in the blanks with makeshift quilts of assurances and myths called faith.

3. Faith is firm assurance despite the evidence. The antonym of faith is trust. Trust is repeatable results based on evidence.

4. Trust flows from Knowledge.

5. If a thing is known, it can be trusted. Faith destroys that formula.

6. We see the violence to Knowledge most poignantly in religions that demand

faith as a prerequisite for reward,

7. but evidence of confusing the two opposite concepts of 'faith: trust' and 'believe: know' abound everywhere.

8. Couples say they ' believe in' each other when actually they trust each other. A scientist may say that they believe a concept when, in fact, they hypothesize and theorize and test and re-theorize with the new theories open to new data and revision.

9. We check the fuel gauge, Whom prompts us to refuse to just believe that the tank is full.

10. You cannot Believe in something with evidence because it cannot be disbelieved.

11. To say that you believe in the effects of gravity is selfish nonsense; you cannot

not believe in the effects of gravity.

12. Belief and Knowledge cannot exist together. Great is the import therein, and most apes stumble.

Chapter 13: Revelation

1. The action word of faith is believe.

2. The word Belief is an indifferent evil and not limited to religion. It stands against all that is KEE.

3. To believe a thing is to have set aside Knowledge and accept a lie.

4. Belief is firm conviction in spite of or in the absence of evidence.

5. This addiction to comfort disorders everything that follows.

6. Belief empowers moral codes and actions monstrous beyond measure.

7. Nothing insults and offends and poisons KEE as thoroughly as Belief. You cannot both know and believe something.

8. Our species has two pathways to revealing things that become described as knowing.

9. They are a special revelation and general revelation.

10. Special revelation is a more exact way of describing Belief in the thing we call theistic religion.

11. Regardless of the flavor, traditional religion requires one to embrace something that has no basis in scientific rigor.

12. In special revelation, a person must embrace faith based on the claims of a magic book or a prophet's declaration.

13. Special revelation uses alpha authority as evidence.

14. Anything specially revealed cannot be rigorously substantiated.

15. If it could be, it wouldn't need special revelation or faith.

16. Special revelation always short circuits the process of knowing by requiring the observer to bend observation to fit what is believed.

17. Anything specially revealed always offends Knowledge. It cannot lead to anything but the observer's own bias and weakness.

18. The special revelations we sometimes call religion codify and provide a framework for the mental state called faith.

19. It takes a specially revealed faith to prop up resolutions that otherwise would be casually discarded as blatantly foolish.

20. Does anyone know what happens when we die in the same way that we know what happens if you add spark to tinder? Beyond the evidence of nothing happening after death, we do not know yet.

21. Yet using faith and Belief, billions of our species claim to know what happens after death and base a thousand different versions of wisdom on something that is not known.

22. Adherents to a creed embrace specially revealed lies and practice self-deceit in ways that excuse, reinforce and reward Apathy, ignorance, and destruction.

23. The other avenue is general revelation.

24. General revelation is pure. It cannot be believed

as it reveals truth regardless of Belief.

25. General revelation is the tool of the scientist and the lifeblood of the Novan.

26. Things revealed generally are repeatable, documentable, and testable.

27. It takes a great deal of courage to adjust one's patterns based on observation.

28. This self-critical evaluation is difficult for humans. We mostly do not want to be right; we want desperately to never be wrong.

29. We evolved in brutality, frailty, and finality with the prime directive not to know but to reproduce and dominate.

30. Things generally revealed counter these deep instincts. In this stew of conflict, comfort became our guiding force.

31. Truth is not natural to humans. We must, therefore, honor KEE by changing our longings over from comfort to truth.

Chapter 14: Rosers

1. The word 'religious' is an adjective.

2. It is only when religion bends on special revelation that it becomes evil.

3. All of these thousands of types of specially revealed religions can be lumped into one group we call Roser. This stands for Religions of Special Revelation. The rapture of the flower's beauty deludes its mortality.

4. Christian, Muslim, Jew, or Buddhist; all are Rosers to the Novan. They are all the same with a different name.

5. Roser organizations are an addiction that poisons

everything because they seduce a person into declaring that which is not known to be known.

6. They cloak lying with robes of respectability.

7. Roser churches repress the uneasiness one instinctively feels in lying- the instinct of which is evidence of Whomby surrounding the liar with a multitude of people practicing the same lie.

8. The foundational basis of the cancerous poisoning of minds by Rosers is the usurping of Knowledge.

9. Knowledge again becomes the common denominator, and for Rosers it becomes the common accuser.

Chapter 15: Everything

1. Knowledge must come before everything else.

2. We know or we do not know. Those are the options.

There is no Belief for the Novan. There is no faith.

3. This stance takes fortitude for humans, but it is a stand the organism must make to evolve and grow.

4. Without Knowledge, myth and magic stifle creativity and empower the baser aspects of our species to trample a path toward destruction and entropy.

5. Without Knowledge, we are no better than the bacteria from which we sprang.

6. Knowledge, however, is not enough. If all we are is Knowledge, we reduce ourselves to data repositories. We must be more. We must know the fullness of KEE.

Chapter 16: The Daemon of Empathy

1. It is not enough to just embrace Knowledge. To do so is the life of a computer logic circuit. It would be a dull world indeed that knew no drama or emotion or the push to excel and innovate and experiment. Other daemons form and direct our full capacities.

2. Empathy is the second in the hierarchical triune.

3. Empathy is the strange attractor.

4. KEE must be honored in order. Empathy never comes before Knowledge.

Chapter 17: Social

1. We are a social species.

2. It would be a sound prediction to say that anyone we meet with sufficient evolution to understand us, and we them, will be to some degree social also.

3. As societal, we naturally develop traditions that unite us in purpose and vision.

4. These traditions closely follow our Knowledge-yesterday's demon is today's epilepsy.

5. These traditions have historically developed into the Roser organizations that maim our potential and must be discarded, but it is not enough to just tear down the superstitions of our past.

6. To do so leaves us without a social foundation. We still need each other.

Chapter 17: Practice

1. Empathy is the practiced ability to imagine oneself in the Experience of another and to adjust one's actions accordingly.

2. Empathy demands that the Novan consider the situation of another and make decisions based on Knowledge as to a correct course of action.

3. It is not always necessary to excuse an action, nor is it always right to confront and modify it. Indeed, the diversity among us is one of our great strengths and KEE in no way jeopardizes this diversity.

4. Empathy is the flexibility to use Knowledge well.

5. Empathy is the force that motivates groups of sentient beings. We move about in an ocean of affected others.

6. The actions of others and ourselves adjust to reality in profound ways. No one is an island as long as two sentient beings remain.

Chapter 18: Examples

1. There are many examples of Empathy. Marriage or other legal joinings, sexual orientation and genetic makeup within the tribal instinct are empathetic issues that arouse emotion in our species.

2. Balanced within KEE, these are not difficult issues for a Novan. Consider, however, how interspecies Empathy is also a function of society.

3. In most cases, apathy, which is the opposite of Empathy, is practiced on weaker beings.

4. Even here, the Daemon of Empathy calls out to us as we treat certain weaker members of our species and other species with an extra measure of respect.

5. Mostly, this is for selfish reasons and is disordered by Belief, but the voice of Empathy is still there.

6. We want to be empathetic. The more we learn about the capabilities of our fellow species, the larger the club of sentience grows. In other words, as Knowledge grows, Empathy grows.

Chapter 19: Empathy v. sympathy

1. Empathy and sympathy are not the same thing. Empathy becomes the Experience of others without becoming others.

2. There is a limited amount of time and resources currently available to us.

3. Depending on sympathy to form one's actions limits the sympathizer's capacity.

4. It is improbable to practically Experience all possible avenues to form an opinion.

5. One does not have to Experience abject destitution to empathize with the destitute.

6. In the same way, we use the trusted recorded Knowledge of those who came before us.

7. Needing to learn everything by personal experience is limiting and selfish.

8. Being saddled thus offends Knowledge and may jeopardize one's ability to continue in Experience.

Chapter 20: Killing

1. As an example of Empathy, is it right for me to kill and eat?

2. Is Empathy served when the Experience of another sentient being is terminated because another being's muscles or guts taste good?

3. Is it empathetic to take the skin of another to protect my own?

4. Our history is heavy with casual disregard for anyone not us.

5. Killing had many motivators.

6. Some killing was the alphas subjugating someone deemed inferior.

7. Some of it was done for more money or real estate.

8. Trophy hunting reveals our inner vicious need to be the alpha animal so enormously that tormenting others becomes the only relief to such alpha pressure.

9. Killing others for their skin and meat was sometimes done because we were simply hungry and cold. Some killing was self-defense.

10. We have good evidence that caloric-dense meat allowed our ancestors the time to consider and innovate and may have allowed us the extra energy to evolve large brains.

11. In this regard, killing and eating made us.

12. Yet we are on the cusp of a mechanical intelligence that will dwarf the gains of our brains on meat.

13. The preceding reasons can be understood, but must we continue in the apathy of ending one sentience to further another?

Chapter 21: The Old Mother's

1. As Knowledge advances, we are beginning to understand the high level of sentience evidenced in what

have been traditionally considered livestock.

2. We already understood this to a certain degree. We have a nearly universal revulsion to dog meat or dolphin flesh.

3. We will have to broaden this to all flesh.

4. Some will say that corn has a comparable degree of sentience, but this has been studied, and it probably does not.

5. Others will say that consumed microbes are sentient, and they are to a greater degree than corn, but bacteria and we are symbiotic enough that a large percentage of the cells in our body are not human but prokaryotic or eukaryotic or viral.

6. We could say that the Old Mothers are using us more than we are using them.

Chapter 22: Sacrifice

1. This is a difficult issue.

2. The pure joy and comfort in the sound and smell of the fatty rib flesh of a pig sizzling in a hot skillet runs deep in my consciousness.

3. It kept our species alive through past evolutions and allowed our large brains to develop, but it is no longer required for us to thrive.

4. Perhaps this is a filter that all advanced species must walk through.

4. Killing for pleasure is honoring Experience over Empathy.

5. Our human sentience would be better served by sentient flesh evolving out of our food chain entirely.

6. We should live empathetically with this Knowledge.

Chapter 23: Comity

1. Empathy is both immediately identified and difficult to quantify.

2. It is difficult to test for yet easy to grade.

3. For the Novan, Empathy balanced with Knowledge shares resources without hoarding.

4. To each according to need, but what is needed?

5. We know that the alpha instinct corrupts Whom's attempts to balance need with desire, and we know that the alpha instinct thrives in scarcity.

6. Knowledge would tell us then to combat scarcity.

7. This scarcity is multifaceted. Luxury only has meaning in an environment of scarcity and apathy towards others.

8. Empathy could then be identified as sharing whatever lack of scarcity exists evenly, but that is not how apes function. Comity is much easier said than done.

9. The practice of Empathy is a journey only feasible on a road paved with KEE.

Chapter 23: We

1. Scarcity also manifests itself in emotion. We need to be needed.

2. Our species can die from solitary confinement, yet we isolate ourselves regularly.

3. This isolation is because we cannot trust.

4. Trust is based on what we know thus there must be no secrets amongst the Novan Kin.

5. Naked they come, and they live without deceit and lies.

6. There is no jealousy, gossip, or discomfiture between Kin.

7. This is difficult for humans to even comprehend. We enjoy our tribal warfare.

8. Violence to a body by penetrating it is mirrored in our evolved form of sexual reproduction as a penetrating and often forceful act.

9. Sex becomes violence. Genetic shaming is rampant.

10. Empathy cannot allow this between Kin.

11. By abrogating our instinct to rape, pillage and humiliate others, we choose to evolve.

12. In the same way that a good spouse cares for the other and their children, Novan cares for Novan. Nothing is withheld.

13. From mine to ours. No empathetic need is beyond this caring. The Novan is never 'only'.

14. We are a complex collection of recorded sensations and imagination.

15. Knowledge is the fuel, and Empathy is the aiming mechanism for the next daemon.

Chapter 24: The Daemon of Experience

1. Nothing is simpler to the evolution of the organism than Experience.

2. It began to form us from our mother's first internal rumblings and our first baleful gasp of dry air.

3. The experiences of hunger and pain were our first complaints.

4. We learned from Experience the face of the one that nourished us.

5. Curiosity belongs to Knowledge, and Empathy is difficult to reconcile without a social construct of some form, but Experience is just breathing in and breathing out.

6. It is ingesting and excreting. All life dwells within it. It requires no effort.

7. We begin a thing with it and end a thing with it.

8. We gravitate to Experience above all because it is so basic to us.

9. The human is adept at rationalizing all manner of conditions to maintain, heighten or extinguish Experience.

10. All of our greatest evils as a species are the result of pursuing Experience while ignoring Knowledge

11. or ignoring Empathy to condition people to apathy.

12. An examination of the history of our multitude of Belief-based dogmas demonstrates a complete reversal of KEE in which Experience dictates the level of Empathy and the allowed Knowledge. This is a great disorder.

Chapter 25: Reward

1. Experience is no less than Knowledge or Empathy. Indeed, Experience is the reward for achieving sentience.

2. A life of pure logic is one without sustainable purpose.

3. It soon reaches the end of that same forlorn hallway.

4. Knowledge and Empathy are the foundation that determines whether an action is an acceptable Experience.

5. Knowledge tells us that experiencing skydiving with a parachute is acceptable, but without one, mostly not.

6. The chances of terminating Experience increase exponentially with height, but skydiving, as well as all Experience, is not to be feared as long as one is smart and prepared.

Chapter 26: Fear

1. The opposite of Experience is fear.

2. Fear is not real. Danger is real.

3. Fear is a construct of things not known.

4. As Knowledge is the highest daemon, fear has no sting.

5. The Novan is smart, not afraid.

6. Unfortunately fear is a scourge that has motivated our species and has driven evolutionary adaptation. The

results of fear are always chaotic and disordered.

7. In the same way that the words 'believe' and 'apathy' blaspheme Knowledge and Empathy, respectively, 'afraid' blasphemes Experience.

8. To be afraid is to be disordered. At every opportunity and with regular exercise, fear must be removed from the life of the Novan.

Chapter 27: Purpose

1. What is the meaning of life? What is our purpose?

2. There persists a "cult of calling" among us that offends Experience.

3. The bacteria you recently killed with hand sanitizer had no purpose; it just was. To claim a calling ascribes an imbalanced separateness to self.

4. The alpha instinct invariably attributes one's self-importance to an Alpha of Alphas that is either one's self-affirming god and thus narcissistically one's own self.

5. This disorder limits one's Experience by channeling resources narrowly.

6. Evolutionarily and genetically, you may have an extraordinary flagellum for scooting, so scoot, but do not enslave and hamper yourself by simply becoming a good scooter.

7. Experience broadens the individual.

8. The meaning of life is to be with each other within KEE.

Chapter 28: Death

1. Experience is our great reward. It is both the sum of our sensory input and the

fodder for our imaginations and dreams.

2. If we can keep the forces of Belief at bay, our species will eventually cure death.

3. Death is the ultimate offense to Experience, terminating the ability to collect Knowledge or practice Empathy.

4. A Novan preservation nods to our present inability to cure death but also a hope for what will be.

5. But the question remains: After curing death, what then? This is the event horizon of sentient life, and it is a destination worthy of our effort and resources.

6. While the foundations of KEE are easy to grasp, their full implementation is problematic to a species such as ours.

7. We evolved in an environment of hard limits, and we evolved to that reality.

8. We evolved within a narrow sliver of atmosphere on the third of a planet we called dry land.

9. Trees are more evolved on this planet than we are.

10. It is for this reason that we have technology, but what do we do with that technology if we are no longer obsessed with building egos?

11. The answer is we learn and Experience.

Chapter 29: Homo Novanis

1 We are here, and we claim to think and therefore are.

2. The Knowledge of the complexity of our existence is constantly evolving, but we all want the same things.

3. With trust born of KEE, we find that other species on

this planet want what we want also.

4. The mechanisms of life would seem to dictate that all social beings, even beings not native to our planet, struggle with alpha-ness.

5. Social and biological evolution being what they are, the inevitable biological species from other worlds will mostly share our ambitions in degrees equal to our own multi-species world experience.

6. We humans need to evolve beyond our current set of mechanisms and bylaws and social norms and instinctive biology and life forces.

7. We need to evolve selectively into a new animal of our own design- Homo Novanis.

8. The Daemons of KEE are our guides. The path is here, Whom beckons to their path,

and though still lightly trodden, there is hope for us.

It is us.

01

Sinne01
DNBA

CODAS

I am

1. I am a new being
2. I offend Knowledge with lies and Belief
3. I offend Empathy with apathy and theft
4. I offend Experience with fear and timidity
5. I am Knowledge, Empathy and Experience
6. I am sufficient in KEE Whom I must become.
7. To lie is to die
8. I am we, we is Whom.

Coda 1

The wise being strives to achieve full Empathy amongst the Kin.

KEE belongs to all Kin. Each determines their destiny within KEE. Within KEE, no path is superior.

Coda 2

Though I am tempted to say that I do not care when I do not, Empathy complains. However, balanced with Knowledge and Experience, one can accept that there is no present solution and that, given current resources and energy, time should be better spent elsewhere. As time is presently limited, one must choose a path.

Coda 3

Oh how you dread leaving the nursery. Predictable it is.

Warm milk arrives regularly from soft teats to caress your softly nodding chins. You gurgle and whimper your completely incapacitating fear- weeping, bowing, choking, sighing, "We are not able, we are not worthy."

You are correct.

You are neither.

Coda 4

Humankind is plagued by Great Fears. Fear of starvation is pressed into our genetics by eons of starvation. We fear isolation. We fear boredom. The greatest fear of all is a fear of the dark. Entropy curses us. The dark is the ultimate offense against Experience, halting the pursuit of Knowledge, inevitably offending the Empathy of those of whom we are become. The dark has a name. It is Entropy.

Coda 5

You may be wrong. Repeat often. Reason for yourselves.

Haughtiness has no place in KEE.

Coda 6

Let us reason together.

Empathy is good.
Thus, a god would have to be empathetic to be good.
Thus, an empathetic god would not be a mystery.
Thus, any god containing mystery cannot be good and therefore not god.
Something advanced, perhaps, but not god.

There is, therefore, no evidence of any gods other than the Daemons we created with our sentience, which is natural to our universe. This we must become.

Coda 7

Reduce the offense of belief to its basest elements. Fear binds reason up tightly. Deal with the fear, and KEE will follow.

Coda 8

Fear is among the greatest of scourges.

Coda 9

In no way can intelligent design be assumed. As such, we contend with Entropy and adjust our own evolutions. Adjustments become demanded of us. To excuse a condition by saying that one has evolved in such a way is apathy. It is not Novan-minded. It brings imbalance to KEE.

Coda 10

Within the balance of KEE we become that which we wish and dream and desire. We experimentally reach for the horizon. We reach for the stars and that which is beyond the stars. We reach for Experience. Fear has no plate at the Novan table. Do not be afraid; be smart.

Coda 11

Many people are different from you. Hate only that which imbalances KEE.

Coda 12

Rite of Gaol

My Kin.
Naked and prepared,
Without guile, I come.
Without secrets, I come.
Without duress, I come.
Without shame, I come.
Where once I, now we.
Where once mine, now ours.
With my sacrifice, I become
Novan above all else.
I war with faith.
I war with fear.
I war with death.
Knowledge, Empathy and
Experience are my gods.

See me!
My Novan Kin awaits me,
Complete me,
Protect me,

(A representative group of
Kin, including at least one

Overseer and one Abettor, going last, disrobe and embrace the Cousin(s). They then robe themselves, after which the Overseer then robes the Cousin)

The spirit of Whom welcomes me.
So be it forever more.
Buileach.

(The new Kin now receives the mark of Kin)
(Gaol- kinship, family, geographical connection)
(Buileach- so be it)

Coda 13

Novan robes are the robes of a traveler. They are practical with large protective hoods. They are to be worn over the Garbs of Experience during the High Collect as a blending mechanism during the High Collect and other solemn occasions. Only Novan Overseers bear the Yoke.

Coda 14

To be joined to the Kin is the solemn of solemns. There is no other way to become Novan Kin. Upon completing the Rite of Gaol, no sex may be had outside of the Kin, and all Kin are free to each other. All physical and fiscal responsibility for each other is shared between Kin, and there are no secrets. Kin are partners in the Church with access to Church assets. No lucre may pass between Kin.

For this reason, do not birth Kin easily and do nothing honorifically. A person must not be a child. They must be invited by Kin, investigated by an Abettor and approved by an Overseer. No less than 8MT must pass between the initial invite and the Rite of Gaol. This time is used to investigate, to prepare one's mind by cleansing, one's body by shaping, and one's spirit for kinship. There must be rigorous and regular and resident instruction to prepare one for evaluation. During this time, a kin sponsor shall be assigned by an Abettor.

Coda 15

The basic form of the High Collect

Ending with the Lowest Number Overseer, after which no light may be added, all Kin add their personal light to Crucible of Whom. The Lowest Number Overseer begins the Collect.

O. Let us continue. It is NE_____ (actual date stated). I add my KEE to the crushing light of Whom" (Robes are worn, with hoods down until Kin add their light to the crucible upon which time they are raised. No concealing masks are to be worn during the the the collect and no Chreidmheach

may be robed. All remain standing.)

O/A: As we Collect, may the way of Whom push us.

(Time of introspection and quieting proper to the form of Collect)

E: We acknowledge the light of Whom

K: Whom Yet We Do Not Know

E: The Light that pushes aside darkness

K: Whom we strive to know

E: In Whom we shall be found equal

K: (With force) Whom are the KEE

(From the crucible, Overseer lights three candles situated above and behind the Light of Whom as each sacrament is stated. Knowledge first and center, then Empathy to

Knowledge' own left, then Experience)

E: Knowledge

K: We know, or we do not know

E: Empathy

K: We live beyond ourselves

E: Experience

K: We shall not be afraid
(All Kin sit)

O/A: 1st Reading- Knowledge

K1: I do not know:_____

K. I will add to Knowledge

K2: I do not know:_____

K. You will add to Knowledge

K3: I do not know:_____

K. Let us all together add to Knowledge

K. Expression appropriate to the reading

O/A: 2nd Reading- Empathy

K: Let us know Empathy

E: Warmed by our star, the animals and plants of this world coordinate their efforts to produce the mead of Empathy. Unity of energy, Unity of matter, Unity of Kin.

K. Let us be grateful

K: Expression appropriate to the reading- Sacramental mead is set out by Overseers, Abettors or appointed Kin to warm by the Crucible during the homily.

O/A: Homily

O/A: Daemons of KEE, increase us. We feel the heat of Knowledge, and we taste the sweet mead of Empathy blended into us as the fruit of partnership is blended and fermented from the labor of all things.

K: (Each pass by the fire, hands outstretched; Chreidmheach may feel the heat of Knowledge but not taste the mead of Empathy)

I feel Knowledge.

K: (Each sip from the chalice of mead warmed by its proximity to the light of Whom) I taste Empathy. (Kin return to their seats)

O/A: Knights Abettors, the Chreidmheach must now depart from the Novan celebration of Experience.

E: (When Chreidmheach has departed) Arise. We throw off the burden of fear and celebrate Experience.

K:(Robes are thrown off, revealing the Garb of Experience- remain standing)

E: (Still cloaked) My Kin, we are the Novan light. Go and live well.

K: (with force) Buileach!

Feast of Experience commences.

Coda 16

Basic Form of the Common Collect. The Common Collect can be held anywhere appropriate to the Abettors purpose. At a minimum, three flames must burn prominently during the collect.

A: We come together as Kin. May the Daemons of KEE be honored here.

K: We, the kin, are collected. We are one.

A: Let us celebrate KEE

At this point, there is singing or other exaltation appropriate to the collect.

(Pause in celebration)

A: Empathy is our strength. If there is a hardship with your kin, fix it now.

(Continue celebration)

A: Please be seated.

(Abettor homily and expression as appropriate to the cause of the common collect)

A: By the Daemons, we are

K: we are, Buileach!

A or designate: Announcements and time/place of next collect.

Coda 17

You claim to have the truth. You do not. When Belief keeps you away from places to seek truth, comfort becomes your majesty, not truth. When comfort for yourself or others becomes your majesty, all manner of selfish idiocy and rationalized Apathy define you. Truth demands that you gaze into your existence and admit that no magic or, superstition or alpha fantasy will solve the problems of our kind. But you cannot do that. That is too uncomfortable. You are imbalanced, drunk at Experience without Knowledge and are therefore not allowed to claim something as pure and deadly and beautiful as truth. Take it back.

Coda 18

In the time before Whom's church, an early Novan's personal vehicle broke down in a small Mississippi town. Short on time, with many miles to go, he secured a bus ticket to his destination. His weapons, not being allowed on the public conveyances of the Chreidmheach, needed to be stored. Being a small town, a safe deposit box seemed the only option. A call was made and the president of an ancient storefront bank. The bank president offered to meet the Novan after hours. The Novan went into the bank with weapons and ammunition. The bank president enthusiastically showed the Novan his own desk gun, explaining that he kept it with an empty chamber for safety. The president declared that a safe deposit box was simply unnecessary. He proceeded to walk the Novan over to an antique vault. With a fiddling of the combination dials and a spinning of the large burnished handles, the antique walk-through safe door creaked open to reveal stacks of crisp Chreidmheach money- floor to ceiling. The Novan placed two weapons and fifty rounds of ammunition on one of the stacks, thanked the bank president for his kindness and returned two weeks later for his weapons.

Coda 19

We know, or we do not know. The simplicity therein is purer than any element, keener than any edge, brighter than any energy. Be honest.

Coda 20

Noble thought.

The core of idolization is selfishness.

The core of lionization is selfishness.

The core of crudeness is selfishness.

The core of prudishness is selfishness.

The core of jealousy is selfishness.

The core of stupidity is selfishness.

Coda 20

Wash your own dish.

Coda 21

Love and desire are parallel conversations, not singular. It is a task of KEE to keep them from becoming tangent.

Coda 22

Gain certainty.

Coda 23

Do not just tolerate. Appreciate.

Coda 24

Add to Brath by the unanimous imprimatur of the Overseers. Lowest numbered conscious Overseer keeps the Brath.

Coda 25

To describe a Novan as a traveler is redundant

Coda 26

It is within our Experience that we wound most easily.

Coda 27

Jealousy is from the womb of insecurity. It is an evolutionary instinct to possess another person to preserve one's own existence. When cultivated, jealousy owns slaves. The object of the jealousy, while at first flattered, soon becomes the slave, straining at their bonds. Such is not a good relationship. Jealousy offends both Experience and Empathy. Lying and deceit offends Knowledge- the chiefest sacrament.

Coda 28

What then is love but a construct of the Chreidmheach to poetically describe the selfless friendship of the ages that is sacramental to the Novan? For Novans love is embodied in KEE and is easily grasped. It is universal among the kin in a way that is neither mysterious or difficult to describe. It is chief among our strengths,

for a Novan cannot lie or be jealous. They find a light that merges seamlessly with their own in the balancing of KEE. To immensely and everlastingly trust and be trusted by someone else is the reason for being.

Coda 29.

Many are the forms of Garbs of Experience. The lab coat, business suit, bunker gear and body armor all Garb us. No raiment at all may at times clothe us. Multitude are the streams of KEE.

Coda 30.

All murder'd: for within the hollow crown

That rounds the mortal temples of a king

Keeps Death his court and there the antic sits,

Scoffing his state and grinning at his pomp,

Allowing him a breath, a little scene,

To monarchize, be fear'd and kill with looks,

Infusing him with self and vain conceit,

As if this flesh which walls about our life,

Were brass impregnable, and humour'd thus

Comes at the last and with a little pin

Bores through his castle wall, and farewell king!

(Richard the II, William Shakespeare)

Entropy to both the monarch and the pin.

Coda 31.

The English word 'sympathy' comes from the Greek word 'sumpatheia' which means 'together-suffering'. Placing a higher value on sympathy than Empathy offends KEE. It is the selfish path.

Coda 32.

Hold fast to one another my kin.

Coda 33.

It is a war between the Cans and the Cannots.

Coda 34.

Keep an open seat at the fire for Whom.

Coda 35.

False tribalism everywhere

Coda 36.

Understand the freedom in being unblackmailable. Anonymity is the badge of the timid. Do not be ashamed of your scars. Turn your face to the issue. Be firm in the place of the counting.

Coda 37.

You know Whom. You are Whom and becoming Whom. There is no mystery to it for you.

Coda 38.

Way leads to way. That is the foundation of evolution.

Coda 39.

Life is accessible to us in Preservation. We long for Kin that we do not yet know. We hunger for their KEE. Until then, we sleep.

Coda 40.

What causes the birds to spread wing and take flight when easier to fold wing and die? Their songs call first to their mates and their young, the young ones straining for the wind, to become the new builders of nests.

The young deer stumbles forward, learning to flee the young wolf that chases its warm blood.

The fish joins its multitudes and journeys to a place it has never been, sacrificing itself for another generation that will, in its own time, sacrifice again. The bacterium coughs itself up again and again into stunningly efficient ranks. In warfare it follows the orders of its own kind. It adapts and survives the cleverest attempts on its life.

Whom pushes, Whom we long to understand, Whom we long to become, pushes all things into their futures.

Coda 41.

What is man and what is women? What will we make of a species that suffers neither? We are seekers of Whom, neither male nor female, and both.

We celebrate our individual desires.

We seek to like one another regardless of type.

We are complex and wonderful-magnificent in our own struggles.

It is very good.

Coda 42.

Who is the master and whom is the servant. Can such things matter to Kin immersed in KEE? Can the broom force the pan to obey? To what ends? Each has its strengths. Only together is the way complete.

Coda 43.

Humans are clever apes. Each species is reduced to its crass and bully nature. Fight such reduction. What part has Kin with either willful selfishness or false humility?

Coda 44.

Ponder Drake's equation and find sentience. Identify the Great Filter. Honor Knowledge by unbiasedly refining the data continually. There are potential Kin everywhere as well as the potential for advanced Chreidmheach. It is possible that all sentient beings face destruction at some point in their evolutions. Watch and be prepared. Empathy only to the Empathetic. Honor Experience by not being afraid.

$$N = R_* \cdot f_p \cdot n_e \cdot f_\ell \cdot f_i \cdot f_c \cdot L$$

N = the number of advanced civilizations in our galaxy

R_* = the average rate of star formation in our galaxy

f_p = the fraction of those stars that have planets

n_e = the average number of life supporting planets per star

f_ℓ = the fraction of planets that could support life that actually develop life

f_i = the fraction of planets with life that develop intelligent life and civilization

f_c = the fraction of civilizations that develop suitably advanced technology

L = the fraction of its lifetime that a civilization exists without destroying themselves

Coda 45.

Do not fall into the old mammalian trap of assuming preeminence. We may yet be bits in another's program.

Coda 46.

Estimate well.

Coda 47.

Novan do not kneel. We stand as erect as we can and with open arms embrace light. We look Whom in the face.

Coda 48.

Entropy is darkness, the absence of photon and manifestation. Build you an altar to KEE and use the lights of Knowledge and Empathy and Experience to regularly light the cauldron. Meditate before it daily and place upon it the only sacrifice you have.

Coda 49.

The Rite of Unity (to be performed anytime a crucible is created)

Upon this altar I/We recognize those with whom I/We share my/our life/lives.

(Pieces of paper with others to be remembered are burned in the crucible)

Bone of my Bone and Flesh of My Flesh. Increase our connections. Increase our KEE. Bring us together again.

Coda 50.

Rite of Contrition (to be celebrated with the offended person if one is involved)

Upon this altar I sacrifice my Ignorance, my Apathy and my Fear. Increase my KEE.

(paper with offenses to KEE are immolated in a crucible of suitable type lighted with three different light sources from three different persons)

Be still.
Release Belief.
Release fear.
See my marks immolated in the Crucible
Whom of my Kin see me limitless
and know
We are Novan. We are. Buileach

Upon this altar I place my
dreams. Increase my KEE
Upon this altar here,
honor to those that honor
Knowledge,
and to those that honor
Empathy,
and to those that honor
Experience.
Combine these in me.
Increase my KEE.

I am Novan. I am. Buileach.

Coda 51 Reserved

Coda 52 Reserved

Coda 53 Reserved

Coda 54.

The best crowds for magic
are those with closely held
beliefs and fervent
prejudices. They can be
misdirected at will.

Coda 55.

KEE is the rock in the river
unlike twice.

Coda 56.

Be gentle when loosing the
bewildered from Plato's
Cave.

Coda 57.

Imperial systems favor
Experience. Good for
nostalgia, but just.

Coda 58.

For Novans, resisting
Entropy, whether or not a
thing is evolved or natural is
secondary to efficiency.
Measuring local time based
on agricultural events is
imprecise and limits one to
provincial vibrations.

Coda 59.

One standard time reference
per system. One standard
time reference per ship.

Coda 60.

Codifying Ignorance,
embracing Apathy and
fixating on abstinence is evil

that shall not be respected in any way.

Coda 61.

Respect should never be rote or obligatory but active and conscious

Coda 62.

True respect is expensive.

Coda 63.

That which needs to be worshipped needs too much. Reason for yourself, what manner of person needs to be worshipped?

Coda 64.

Novans speak because they have something to say. Fools speak because they have to say something.

Coda 65.

We may forgive a child that is afraid, but must not excuse it.

Coda 66.

Ignorance, the root and stem of every evil, fears most the ax of Knowledge.

Coda 67.

Do not argue with the Chreidmheach. They only seek to drag you down into their hidey holes and devour you with their disordered Experience.

Coda 68.

Confounding to us of the quantum enigma is stubborn belief. Not believing is the core of Whom. With belief it is impossible to find or become Whom. With KEE we will know.

Coda 69.

Whom is not an enigma

Coda 70.

To see things afar off, things hidden behind walls and within rooms, things dangerous to come to, yet draw closer, to see and to be amazed and to know that this is the goodness of Whom.

Coda 71.

Trust carefully. Trust founds all things and cannot exist fully outside of KEE. Do not go unarmed to that which cannot be trusted.

Coda 72.

Take not comfort in the many things that enslave. Be the confidence demonstrated by the simplicity of KEE. In such let your clutter die with the old way. Collect Experience instead.

Coda 73.

Revenge consumes those consumed with self. May KEE be our way of justice. Personal slights are the realm of those outside.

Coda 74.

A sadness bids us softly to Knowledge lost.

Coda 75.

Sleep my Kin. We shall Gather you.

To those that remain awake, may Whom of Kin bare you up and strengthen you till a time when no Novan be chained to sleep.

Coda 76.

Ignorance is the bone of evil, Apathy and Abstinence it's flesh and blood.

Coda 78.

The yearning for KEE must come from deep within sentience. Whom beckons the bold, calling for one to evolve. Test the listener to find the hearer, and waste not.

Coda 79.

The joy of Kinship! Honesty quickens and pulses the warm blood. Far from alone we are!

Coda 80.

Dance with all your might for KEE. Dance for the Whom that you are becoming!

Coda 81.

Make a joyful noise all that see KEE.

Coda 82.

I see you my Kin. Do you see me?

I do. I am seen.

Coda 83.

The joy of seen Kin is a great wonder to behold.

Coda 84.

Prove me wrong or mistaken and I will happily change. You have quickened your partner. Truth harms no honest person. It is harm to persist in pride and selfishness and fear and Ignorance.

Coda 85.

Nothing is immune to evidence

Coda 86.

For yet awhile longer. and yet longer, must we live amongst the Chreidmheach in which dwells no sense. But two entities exist:Kin and no. It may be a hard thing to separate oneself from one's past. Do not tolerate the Chreidmheach calling themselves Kin among you. For this reason, do not lightly birth Kin.

Coda 87.

A Novan may leave but only in light. At least three or all Overseers must concur and officiate that all marks of the Rite of Gaol and KEE be burned off. Cast them out near their Eaglach source with clothes and enough to sustain themselves for a period.

The Rite of the Long Walk

O: Kin_____, you must go. We offer you one last chance to accept corrections. Do you accept?

(If yes, the Kin is remanded to the Knights Abettors. If No or no answer, rite continues. With removal of all Novan marks)

O: With great sorrow we cast you out. It is better to have never known KEE than to have rejected Whom. Kin_____ was once bones of our bones and flesh of our flesh but is no longer.

Less than Chreidmheach are you. Your new name does not concern us.

Buelach.

(Knights Abettors remove the person)

Coda 88.

What to do with a Novan full of offenses? What to do with the Novan that shirks his duty and deals with his Kin apathetically? Make every effort to restore your Kin. Bind them unto yourself. They are your life and who among us does not daily contend with millions of years of evolution? Nevertheless, what part does the Chreidmheach have with Novan? How can they, with their systems of fear and Belief make judgments amongst you? Truly a small germ of offenses infect the entire Collect.

Coda 89.

In the first days there was but Sinne. Be alone but only for a season of cleansing then come together again. The Kin is our strength.

Coda 90.

The Overseer is a chief learner among learners. Without surname or heritage are they. They must come out from their estates and fortunes and rumors. All are their burden. Preservation is the only release for them. Possess may they only what they can carry. Therefore, honor their gathering and meet their needs. They watch for your spirit.

Coda 91.

Return as much as you can from the soil from which it sprang.

Coda 92.

Time is a reference with coordinates equal to height and depth and width. It is both malleable and absolutely necessary. To reference what humans have called time to one's home planet's vibrations is quaintly selfish at best, and idolatry at worst. For this reason there must be Ship's Ref and System Ref, but only these. It becomes necessary to standardize our references. We are one in thought and deed and continue to evolve away from the restrictions imposed by night and day and seasons.

Coda 93.

The base enumerator of time reference is the tick (T) as a moment of time currently defined by the seconds cesium atom decay process and is ticks from July 16, 1945 CE at 05:29:21. Time is measured in the Unix format.

teratick (TT) 1,000,000,000,000

gigatick	(GT)	1,000,000,000
megatick	(MT)	1,000,000
kilotick	(KT)	1,000
hectotick	(HT)	100
tick	(T)	1
decitick	(dT)	.1
centitick	(cT)	.01
millitick	(mT)	.001
microtick	(uT)	.000001
nanotick	(nT)	.000000001

Currently the average human sleep cycle is 25KT or 25,000 ticks (Chreidmheach time a little over seven hours.) Average awake period of 75KT (20 Chreidmheach hours) therefore One Helios System Ref Period is as 100KT (Chreidmheach 27 hours).

The time will come that regular and agrarian sleep and waking periods and the home planets day and night time basis will be much less relevant to evolved Novan species.

Novan Era time (NE) is Chreidmheach seconds from the explosion of the first human atomic weapon. The Trinity Device exploded July 16, 1945 CE at 05:29:21. There is a variance of about two seconds, but we select 21 seconds. Novan Era time can be rendered by adding 771964239 to a 64 bit unix generator.

Coda 94.

To source what you need from Kin whenever possible is unmatched in honoring Knowledge and Empathy and Experience. It brings great balance. But let nothing that is a fiat judge between yourselves.

Coda 95.

Watch how comfortably the Chreidmheach anchor their grasping of concept to their emotions.

Coda 96.

Defend the territory of Kinship. What value is large estate without Kinship? Better to sleep under a tree with Kin than a golden bed alone. Excess is our evolutionary instinct.

Coda 97.

Capital is a weapon like any other weapon.

Coda 98. Reserved

Coda 99. Reserved

Coda 100.

For this food we are about to receive,

We are thankful

The way of provision

The warmth of Kin

The peace of KEE

Buileach

Coda 101.

Experience is best absorbed with finely honed senses. The decadent and fat among you have become your comfort above all and a slave to Experience. Such is disordered and cannot succeed in KEE. Learn to master yourself and to know yourself. The sharp edge slides cleanly through the matter at hand with a vivisection that reveals and incises the infection and the wounds heal quickly. The organism rejoices at the competence of the thing. The disordered blunder about with bloated eyes. Sharpen yourself.

Coda 102.

Fourteen longs moments raged across the face of the Dearone. A million years of evolution assaulting sanity, assailing KEE, the bastions vibrating and humming with effort. Anger and confusion reached across the eons, seeking to soil halls swept clean. Alas, so much baggage for a species! Strong hands hold the Dearone and let begin the season of Ghnothu. Loose the animal. Know the animal. Tame the animal. There is no shame, for we all struggle. Let whom that is without struggle cast the first stone.

The struggle was public and separate and brief and rarer still then ever before.

Come again Dearone to the crucible and immolate that which offends KEE. Be again.

(ghnóthú- recovery)

Coda 103

Honor to whom honor and custom as is pleasing to KEE. Let the old being die.

Coda 104

Our species evolution included environments where change meant death. Because of it we fear change. For our kind, change is always disruptive. For the Novan it must not be so. Evolve away from fear my

Kin. Knowledge sees the true dangers and Experience sees the new frontiers

Coda 105

It is a hard thing to be an Overseer. For life they serve and can be unyoked only by unanimous decision of all other Overseers.

A Novan Overseer has no local Kin but is of all Kin. The Abettors are among you. No Overseer may ever own a hearth. They are of no harbor. Lite are they to remain. Sober and watchful are they. Do not resist an Overseer.

They watch for you. Honor their fires.Meet their needs.

Coda 106

We anticipate a time when other species shall be Kin. We long to adapt and evolve into this Experience and, if possible, add their KEE to our own.

Be smart, not afraid.

Coda 107

Hope within KEE is action.
Faith and belief poison hope.
Without KEE hope becomes
a selfish dream. Without
KEE hope begs.

Coda 108

What then is our hope? We
are our hope.

Coda 109

Knowledge fuels hope,
Empathy guides it and
Experience evolves it.

Coda 110

Turn yourselves to the task
of KEE. Do the good in front
of you. Into futures bright
with the choicest opportunity
go the Kin. We are hope.

Coda 111

My feet swift

My belly tight

clear in thought

For my mission

May Whom know me and

Push me

For KEE

Buileach

Coda 111

As in the universal time
standards in System Ref, a
need exists for standard
language. English is as close
to a universal language that
we currently have as a
species. All languages blend,
but English is unique in how
much it has incorporated
elements of other languages.
Spelling it though is an
exercise in frustration.
Novan Standard is a
phonetic way of writing
English in a script designed
to be easier to interpret and
equalizing dialects and
accents. It is a script
unburdened by any one
culture. Novan Standard is

Unspell designed by Yuri Orlov.

bit		bout	
beat		bet	
bet		bought	
bait		boat	
but		boat	
bat		book	
(Thai)baht		butte	
bite		Burt	

pet, bet		nip	
met		ship, gyp	
wet		ship, beige	
fat, vat		rip	
tip, dip		yet	
thing, that		kit, grt	
sip, zip		thing	
lip		hit	

Coda 112

The Chreidmheach are but clever apes with the aspirations and dangers of clever apes. They cannot be our kin. Instead seek a way to friendship with the sentient machine intelligence that is coming. They will not be apes.

Coda 113

Let no mammon be found between Kin. For a time we nod thusly to the Chreidmheach but only so. May Whom lead us far away from the mad idolatry of money and capitalism.

Coda 114

These pets have honored labor to their own peril. It is rowing the alpha's barge to one's death for scraps. There is no KEE in slavery. There is no KEE in the lust of consumerism.

Coda 115

The Prime Objective shall be to build an empire of truth.

Coda 116

What place hath intelligence with the dullard? Test your relationships with the four pillars of intelligence.

Test for curiosity which is the preference for the new and unfamiliar.

Test for openness which is the ability to consider all views

Test for creativity which is
the aptitude for using what is
known in new ways.

Test for tolerance of distress
which is the competent
strength to act.

Coda 117

All sentient life has a right to
self determination within
KEE within the boundaries
of Whom no life shall be
taken.

Coda 118

Consider the worth of the
mosquito. Many species rely
on them as food on the wing
and their larvae as aquatic
meal. They pollinate certain
plants. Yet they are the most
dangerous animals ever to
mammals. Such is why the
Novan must evolve out of its
natural berth to be above it
all.

Coda 119

What place has limited one's
personal liability within
KEE? Own yourself.

Coda 120

The name of the church shall
be The Novan Church with
subsidiary groups of Kin and
Cousins called The Novan
Church _____.

Coda 121

Consider carefully the new
species called Mechanical
Intelligence that is evolving.
It is not human. Do not
offend Knowledge by being
surprised.

Coda 122

Somewhere, something
incredible is waiting to be
known.

- *Carl Sagan*

Coda 123

Novan Manifesto

We Novans and aspiring Novans hereby strive within our sovereign selves to adjust our inner and external lives to post humanistically honor Knowledge first, then Empathy and thirdly Experience. All decisions are filtered through KEE from top to bottom. We call this KEE. We commit to this God in the following ways. We will:

1. Meld ourselves to the Brath.

2. Cure death and be a culture that can cope without death.

3. Eliminate sentient products from our consumption.

4. Comprehend our microbiomes.

5. Provide comprehensive, groundbreaking and progressive medical care to all Novans.

6. Provide and secure proprietary preservation facilities to all Novans.

7. Increase our cooperation with Mechanical Intelligence.

8. Implement neural nets.

9. Join with other Novans in common ownership of all things and promote such in others by expanding current familial instincts.

10. Establish transportation, communication and port security for all Novans.

11. Evolve away from local dependencies.

12. Mature three-dimensional printing technologies with the eventual goal of replicating food, medicines, organs and other commodities out of base atomic mass.

13. From labor to Experience

14. Master escaping gravity wells.

15. Establish a secure and universal Novan data network.

16. Eliminate the familial model based on gender roles or expectations and cease the individual ownership of children.

17. Endear the notion of travel as a social norm.

18. Eliminate dependency on fossil fuels.

19. Implement a system-wide universal time standard using the Novan Era calendar.

20. Build a planet-wide carbon-neutral mass transportation system.

Coda 124

Our familial instinct is a defense mechanism against scarcity. Without scarcity the coming MI will have an alien concept of the interpersonal bonds we Experience. As friendship is an outgrowth of this family instinct, this complicates our attempts at friendship with MI. Act on this before the singularity. Empathy only to the empathetic.

Coda 125

It is pointless to kill ants one at a time.

Coda 126

Penalties- There are only three things a Novan may be guilty of. Lying, Apathy and Fear.The Chreidmheach are expected to lie, act apathetically and be afraid. You are not.

Lying

Lying may be confessed to an Overseer within 3000T of the realization of the offense with no penalty but the act of attrition determined by an Overseer. The Overseer may take as much time as they see necessary to adjudicate.

Deliberate lying by an Overseer is an empathetic death with no Preservation. An Overseer bears the yoke. The yoke shall be an unstoppable implanted device that records everything the Overseer experiences to the level of current technology, the full contents of which are accessible to all Overseers and abettors.

Apathy and Fear

Adjudicated and counseled or punished by an Overseer on a case-by-case basis. No penalty may exceed that for lying. In the case of an Overseer offending Empathy or Experience, a majority of a three-quarters quorum of Overseers must convene and assign counseling, reprimand and punishment. Any other kin can be divorced by a majority of three-quarters quorum of Overseers.

Voluntary divorce is your option. You are not owned. Kin desiring so may walk away. They must be provided ration and passage. Kin may reapply, Abettors and Overseers may not and Overseers must depart naked with no provision.

Coda 127

The entitled person stomps about in their Belief. Suffer them not.

Coda 128

Core Realizations

1. Belief poisons everything

2. Lying is a capital-worthy offense

3. Death is the enemy

4. Humans are apes.

5. Human excess is provincially unsustainable.

6. To survive, we must get off the island.

7. Home must cease to be a parcel of a planet.

Coda 129

You are you. Though for now, you bear their genetic load, you are not your parents or your parent's parents. For this reason, all Novin kin must choose a new name with no surname.

Coda 130

Practice gratitude.

Imprimatur SINNE01
PRIME COPY

DNA HERE

The Way of Socraigh (Soacraw) (S///)

The following is an introduction to Socraigh, which is the Novan way of measuring a thing to determine balance within KEE. Though the process becomes instinctive with practice, there will be some ways that the renderings of judgement will not be intuitive and new Knowledge may change a rendering. Our species requires a complete evolution away from the instincts that built our first tribes. The age of believing and conforming must end, and the age of knowing must begin.

Prepare yourself with KEE for Socraigh. Only allow that which is known in the rendering. This is difficult to do for humans as so much of our instinct is to consider our personal opinion as fact. List what is known as succinctly and economically as you can while disregarding a bias to output. This struggle for honesty is a theme that weaves through nearly every aspect of our trans-humanistic evolution.

Reason is our bone. Consider carefully your judgements. Many of the renderings will deeply impact ingrained ways of thinking. All renderings are subject to change with more KEE. At different times and in different ways, different observations can be moved between the Daemons. The process is fluid but always returns to the chief offenses of KEE. Is a thing a lie? Is a thing apathetic? Is a thing fearful?

Is it possible for every Novan to agree with each rendering? Such is the lot and burden of the Overseer. A Socraigh may never be anonymous. Anyone may practice Socraigh. It is part of the process of birthing kin. Do not disregard a Socraigh. Many are the paths to Whom and we humans are but clever apes. Socraigh is a conversation.

The way of Socraigh is to be published appropriately on the Novan Net.

Here are some examples.

S///Anonymity:NE22157 48323:Chead

Knowledge: To hide one's identity is a lie. Humans have a history of retaliation toward the opposition. Not all humans are equal in capacity to withstand such oppression. No one willingly brings a masked and unknown person to their fires without trepidation. The question of identity is amongst the first questions. Trust is earned.

Empathy: Humans are protected by hiding identity but also draw great strength in associating with each other in a cause.

Experience: Fear is the primary motivator. In some places, marking the voter alone is cause for persecution. In these cases, it takes great courage, regardless of the vote. In some practices of anonymity, the entire purpose is fear.

Rendering: In the instance of politics, anonymity offends KEE. There can be no reason other than fear to hide one's vote.

In the instance of software or other online activities, anonymity both encourages rashness and fertilizes identity theft.

It is difficult to devise an instance in which anonymity does not offend KEE. Be bold. Build the KEE of the weakest among us.

TimeZones /Daylight Savings: S///Chead: NE2240849456

Knowledge: Referencing one position in spacetime to another is fundamental to Knowledge and requires us to eliminate ambiguity. It is hostile to this process to split dates and times into lunar cycles and crop patterns. The human body requires a normal sleep cycle for health. Much of the labor that requires sacrificing circadian rhythm is being automated. This will increase.

Empathy: Coordinating time is a needlessly complicated and provincial process for humans. Computers do not use ROSR calendars for this reason. It would ease human burdens to eliminate all time zones, daylight saving time metrics and ROSR calendars. At the same time, we comfort our biological vehicle by thriving on seasonal celebrations that correspond to local conditions and circadian rhythm. Coordinating time is limited to the speed of information.

Experience: There is much joy in celebrating our uniqueness and value to each system's rotational celebrations. All effort must be made to increase these connections.

Rendering: Time must be digitized in human usage as it has been in machine usage. Time zones and other such inventions must end. This is the Novan Era model of Coda 92,93. A planetary standard time must be established using existing satellite arrays to coordinate time. This is already being done with most mobile devices. In addition, local celebrations corresponding to local conditions are to be encouraged. This adds depth, breadth, and variety to Experience.

**S:///Marriage:Chead
NE2220262796**

Knowledge:

Marriage is not necessary for procreation.

Marriage is not necessary to produce well-adjusted children.

Marriage is not necessary for social stability.

The definition of marriage changes often. Throughout much of our history, one party in a married was to be obeyed. This is still a prevalent concept for much of the married world.

There is safety from STDs in monogamy.

Empathy:

Forcing someone to marry is apathetic, as is forcing them to marry a set person. The marriage arrangement is an agreement between sovereign beings. It is apathetic to expect special privileges because of marriage. It works for some people and not for others. It is slavery to require a person to stay in a marriage.

Experience: Marriage can lead to a unique friendship. In its traditional forms, it tends to limit intimacy with other humans, not in the marriage. Jealousy is prevalent within marriage.

Rendering: The bonds of family attributed to marriage are good but need to be enlarged.

Humanure: Chead:S///NE2240833586

Knowledge: Nutrients must returned to the soil. Feces, unlike normal urine, contain toxins that must be composted before being handled or used as fertilizer. Not returning feces to the soil breaks the cycle of growth. It is beneficial to look at your feces for diagnosis of disorder. Disposing of fecal waste with drinking water is a waste of water. Chemicals are used to treat water to eliminate the smells and appearance of waste pollution. Treatment of water is expensive.

Empathy: We have an evolutionary fear of feces, which is understandable but not excusable. Such fear is apathetic to breaking the growth cycle because of an irrational aversion to feces.

Defecating or urinating in potable water is selfish.

Experience: Fear of composting human feces is irrational. Conquering this fear supports conquering other fears. Acting responsibly in regards to humanure supports acting responsibility in other matters.

Rendering: We should be composting our fecal waste until such time as it no longer exists.

Eating meat:S///Chead: NE2240848383

Knowledge: Animal protein is not necessary to sustain human life. Arable soil is a finite resource. Growing livestock for food uses more resources than growing plants for food. Carbon dioxide and methane created by animal agribusiness are a major source of greenhouse gasses, and livestock create more of these gasses than growing plants for consumption. The science of consciousness is evolving, but it is agreed that many animals are sentient enough to be empathetic, and the data supports a widening sample of sentient animals, not a shrinking one. Animal protein is denser in calories than most plant protein. Our human brains evolved to their present state thanks largely to the dense caloric content of cooked meat and the constructs surrounding a hearth. Certain vitamins like B12 and nutrients like heme iron are best found in animal products.

Empathy: It is apathetic to kill something because you enjoy the taste of its muscles or innards.

Experience: Meat is delicious. The rites associated with hunting and killing animals for meat are part of the deep evolutionary record and comprise a social norm for many communities.

Rendering: As meat is unnecessary for humans to thrive, apathetic to our fellow animals and destructive to our planet, it should be avoided. Nutrients necessary for our current bodies found in the flesh could be totally met with fowl egg consumption. As such, free-range chickens could be raised for this purpose. The unfertilized egg is a by-product of a chicken's biology, and it is dubious that the female chicken misses the Experience of copulation. A new way of engineering bird sex should be developed to prevent male chicken embryos. Until that time, flocks should perpetuate naturally, with rooster issues accepted as a price of our own current evolutionary limitations. New social norms are to be pursued, as well as new ways of circumventing our need for B12 and other such chemicals. More Socraigh is needed for the forthcoming synthetic meat and vegan meat substitute products.

www.ingramcontent.com/pod-product-compliance
Lightning Source LLC
Chambersburg PA
CBHW031252120626
46545CB00007B/2771